The Scribblings of a Madcap Shambleton

by Noel Fielding

First published in Great Britain in 2012 by Canongate Books Ltd,
14 High Street, Edinburgh, EH1 1TE

Design & Photography by Ape. apeinc.co.uk © Dave Brown, 2011

Additional Photography:
Kerri Fersel Bennett: P. 17
Lliana Bird: P. 8
Andy Brown: P. 48, 49
Nobby Clarke: P. 2, 75, 112, 265
Nigel Coan: P. 233, 260
Gary Moyles: P. 298
Amy White: P. 133

British Library Cataloguing-in-Publication Data. A catalogue record
for this book is available on request from the British Library.

ISBN 978 0 85786 205 1

Reproduction by Syntax, Edinburgh

Printed and bound in Italy by LEGO S.p.a.

www.hooliganartdealer.com

www.apeinc.co.uk

www.canongate.tv

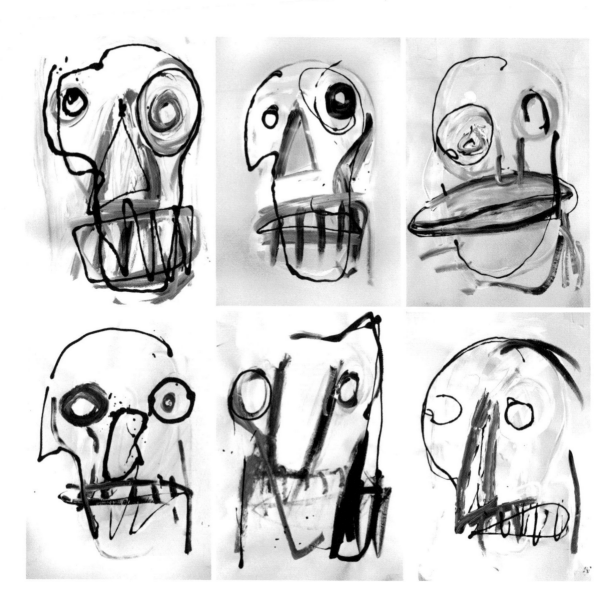

ME AT THE OPENING OF MY
2nd ART SHOW IN GREEK ST.

(A HORROR CLOWN IN A DRESS.)

NOELX

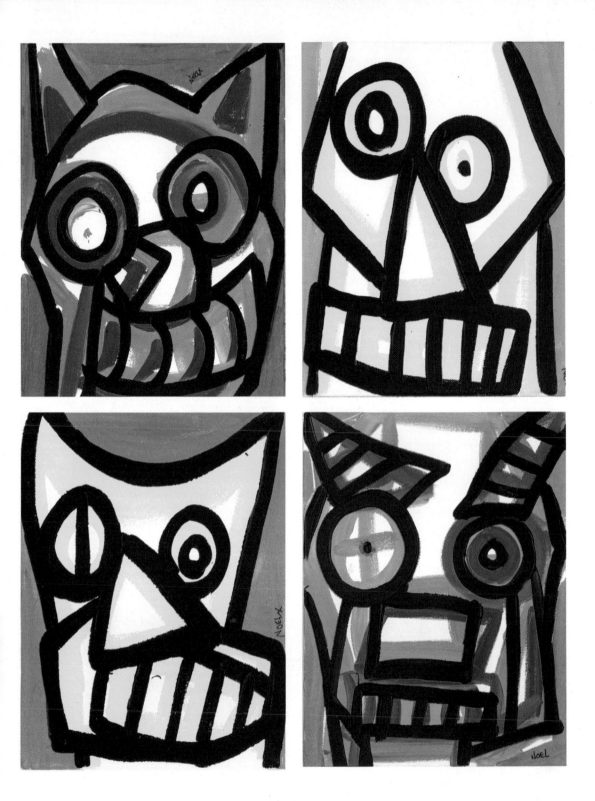

AN ENDORSEMENT

To whom it may concern.

What you have just looked at is not an art book, nor is it a comedy book, or an instruction manual for newlyweds, its not a device for the calculation of tides or a recipe book for the deaf. It is, however, a life saver.

My good friend Fielding sent me a copy of this book to my isolated cabin on Spitzbergen and it kept my sanity intact throughout the long winter days and brought a brilliance and complexion to the endless darkness and bear attacks.

As you have recently discovered, his use of colour and form are second to none, brilliant tones and hues accompany fabulous shapes, such as circles, squares and his favourite, the 'Triangle', the most comical of all the shapes, in fact, I spent many an evening hoisting myself out of troughs of depression laughing at his triangles.

I need not prattle on longer about this remarkable and breathtaking publication as you have, by this stage, finished studying it and are keen to return to your lodgings, however, I will say this.

My good friend Fielding is amongst one of the most specific people in our artistic community and should be welcomed at any cultural get together or creative fund raising event.

Yours forever

Vic Reeves 2011

LIST OF WORKS

All these artworks were produced at some point in the last ten years. Noel can't remember exactly when he did them because he doesn't own a watch. The two things he hates most in the world are food and time.

Noel Fielding has exhibited at Maison Berteaux, The Last Tuesday Society, The Saatchi Gallery and his own bathroom. Work available to purchase at **www.hooliganartdealer.com.**

Thank you
very much...

Dave Brown & his eyes of a kingfisher, Dexter Dalwood, Jim Moir, Lliana Bird, Chiggy & Pat at PBJ,
Jamie, Nick, Norah & all at Canongate, Tania Wade, Daisy & Stanley, Dee Plume, Nobby Clarke,
Louise Lloyd & Violet Mae Brown, Nigel Coan, Ivana Zorn, Gary Moyles, Alison Mosshart, Paul King,
Richard Ayoade, Willy Borrell, Amy & Sergio, Kerri & Danny Bennett, Andy Brown, The Ivy, Christine Cant,
June & Pete, Steve & Syntax Digital, Eddy, Rob & all at BEAR, Paul Holmes & The Velvet Onion gang & all
those who let Noel deface their face, Maison Berteaux, Paul Foot, Belsize Village Delicatessen, Paul Panther,
Andy Kaufman, Ray & Di, Micheal Fielding, Cy Trombley, Henri Rousseau, Johnny Morris, The Silver Apples,
Jaques Brel, Dennis Hopper, Elle Gaitskell for providing the title "You feel as though you know him!",
David Lee Roth, The lady who lent us her black dog, The black dog, Dr Gannis, Nanny Porpoise, Steppenwolf,
Steve Cram, Mark Stafford & Spencer at Staffords, Jean-Michel Basquiat, Picasso, Snitch,
The Baseball Furies, Endless Boogie, ODB, Jack Black and Ben, Shellsuitzombie, Jean Cocteau, Karel Appel,
Jean Debuffet, Don Van Vliet, Mitch Hedberg, 80s Matchbox B-Line disaster, Joan Jet, Jacques Tati,
W.C. Fields, Family Zappa, Courtney Love, Poirot, Beautiful Indian lady at the zoo, Brian Ferry, The Jelly Fox,
The Runaways, The Last Tuesday Society, Secret Peter, Kim Noble, The Guess Who Boys, The Groucho, Jim
Morrison, Elvis, Richard Prior, Vincent Gallo, Richard Brautigan, Sabu the elephant boy, Joey Page, Diamond
Lil, Sam Kinison, Julian Barratt, Syd Barrett, Steve Martin, Harry Nilsson, David Byrne, Dan Clark, Tom
Meeton, Dolly Wells, Little Gay One, Xavier Renegade Angel, Devendra Banhart, Pacman, Brushes App, Joni
Mitchell, The Tiger Spider, Fraser at Nudie Jeans, Morph, Henry, Melvis, Sean, Rach & Rev, Blackie, Rich
Fulcher, The Hawley, Chaz, Tony Hart, Aggers, Kate Bush, Robbie Coltrane, Jodorowsky, Snake Pliskin, Karen
O, Hunter S. Thompson, The Stooges, Keith Haring, Suicide, Ringo Starr, Roger Burns, Norris McWhirter, Roy
Castle, Klaus Kinski, Royal Trux, The Ramones, Mick & Keef, Richard Bird, The Chelsea Hotel, Kev on the
pipes, Zack & Shoosh, Can & Damo Suzuki, Donald Camel, The Human Mistake, The Tiger with Chlamydia,
Tame Impala, Addison Lee, Brian, Paul Gauguin, Vincent Van Gogh, Withnail and I, Everyone who's helped,
supported, influenced, attended, laughed, bought & appreciated. Everyone I've forgotten to thank.
Oh and just one more person....Peter Falk.

Dedicated to the memory of PeterFalk aka Colcembo

This book was Designed, Compiled & most of the Photography is by Dave Brown

Foreword by Dexter Dalwood

(Turner Prize nominee and Noel's first fine-art teacher)

Sometime in the late eighties I walked into Croydon College to teach a BTEC graphic design class their one day a week of 'fine art'. I saw across the room a boy who resembled an Easter Island head, cheeky and kind of keen. I tried to guide him through life drawing (inept), print-making (hopeless), painting (er...what?). But he had such a way with words. He could make the whole class weak with laughter. Scatter-gun sharp in witty comments that could be profound, plain daft and even sometimes generous, though often barbed.

One day he brought in a painting for some half-baked project he was working on. It was a 'version' of Claude Monet's *Houses of Parliament* and I use the word 'painting' lightly, as it was probably the worst I had ever seen a BTEC student do, so bad that it almost flipped into genius. He had left it unsigned. I told Noel it looked more as if it had been done by a Bob Smith than a Monet. And, much to his squealing delight and with his encouragement, I took a brush and crudely wrote 'Bob Smith' in the right-hand corner.

Nearing the end of his course and mine (I quit), Noel did ask for a little advice: 'Should I pursue a future in the arts?'. Not wanting to put him off, I suggested that a career in making people laugh might be more appropriate.

Years later he asked me to go see him perform at the Hen and Chickens, a small pub in Islington (prior to the Boosh going to the Edinburgh Festival). I sat mesmerised in the dark as he displayed some of those extraordinary skills in visualisation and perception I had so carefully nurtured all those years before.

I THINK WHAT DEXTER IS TRYING TO SAY IS I WAS ~~██~~ ~~██~~ THE BEST STUDENT HE EVER HAD!
(HE JUST LACKS MY GIFT FOR WORDS)

Introduction

I remember I was a very shy child, and the thought of school terrified me. My first day was hugely traumatic; our parents were allowed to stay with us for a few hours until we had settled in. My dad was still with me by the afternoon. I can remember the precise moment he decided to slip away; I was in the playground hiding under my blonde fringe, playing a game of 'What's the time, Mr. Wolf?'. He gestured to me to see if it was ok for him to leave. I nodded, tried to be brave and watched my seventies Dad (the image of George Best) slip through the school gates. The next few hours were a blur of snot and tears.

That afternoon the teacher set us the task of drawing some birds for the coming assembly and I relaxed as I sketched bird after bird with speed and ease. At one point I was sketching a golden eagle, and I felt a strong presence behind me. A group of my new classmates were crowded around my tiny desk, gawping at my sketch of an eagle. As my teacher strode towards me I thought I was in big trouble. Maybe I had dreamed up this task and we were supposed to be drawing fish. I froze and hid behind my Lady Di fringe once more. I wanted real birds to fly through the window and carry me off to a land with no schools. Much to my surprise the teacher smiled and announced, *'Noel is a fine artist, and will draw birds for the rest of the class to colour in.'* Everyone seemed pleased with this outcome and as I looked around at the other children's drawings, I quickly realised why. There were fat birds with big eyes, small birds with square beaks and one bird that resembled a phone wearing shoes. I had always drawn, every day as long as I had held a pencil, and just assumed everyone else had too. It was like being famous for an afternoon. I made lots of friends and it helped me overcome my shyness and fear of school. Art had saved me and helped me fit in.

As the term progressed we found out what other children were good at – football, fishing, dancing and lying – but art was always my saving grace. I even charged ten pence for drawings at playtime to buy sweets with after school. Comedy didn't come until much later for me. I've always tried to combine the two things, art and comedy, and couldn't make a choice between the two. It was always my ambition to make comedy with an art-school slant, and art that could be funny instead of po-faced.

I hope I have managed to achieve that in this book, and I hope you enjoy it. If you don't, just do what I would and draw and paint over it.

Noelx

'Salamando'

"OOOH   OOOOOOOH
I SAW HIM IN THE WINDOW."
OOOOOOOOO OO H
YOU'RE SUCH A SALAMANDO OOOH!

COME ON PEOPLE
THESE ARE FOR

BRIAN

YOU LOOK TOO FAST!

VAN GOTH : PAUL! PAUL! PAUL! PAUL!

PAUL : & WHAT?

VAN GOTH : WHY HAVE YOU PAINTED IT SO FLAT?

PAUL : THAT'S HOW I SEE IT.

VAN GOTH : Look PAUL IT'S MORE COMPLICATED THAN THAT. WHAT DO YOU SEE WHEN YOU LOOK AT MY WORK?

PAUL : YOU PAINT TOO FAST.

VAN GOTH : You Look Too FAST !

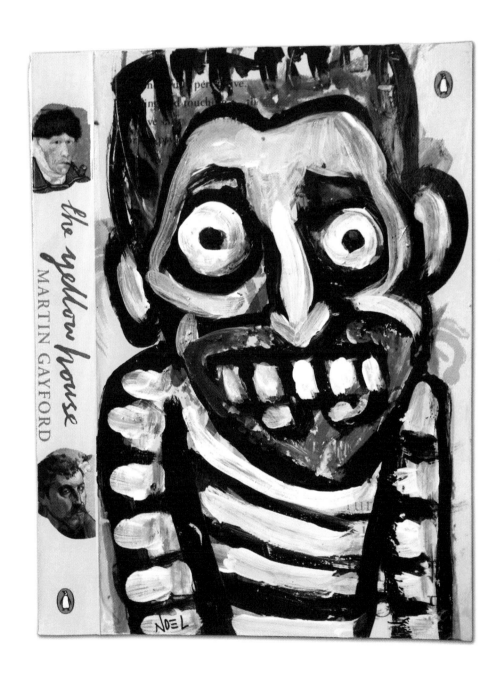

the yellow house

MARTIN GAYFORD

NOEL

HAND PICKED BY MORPH

23

CROSS IT. BOBBY

TRADITIONAL GHOST
Vs
ZAPPA GHOST

FINAL SCORE 3 . 1

TRADI
GH

BEZZIE MATES

TWO FRIENDS ON SKATES.

BUNNY : I LOVE YOU. ~~.~~

ANGRY SHAPE : I LOVE YOU. ~~MY BEST FRIEND~~

BUNNY : WHY THEN ARE YOU PURSUING ME
OVER THIS CLIFF ?

ANGRY SHAPE : I ALWAYS ~~XXXX~~ HURT WHAT I
LOVE.

BUNNY : FAIR ENOUGH. WE'VE ALL GOT ISSUES.

allos
T. Shirt
VALENCIA #4388

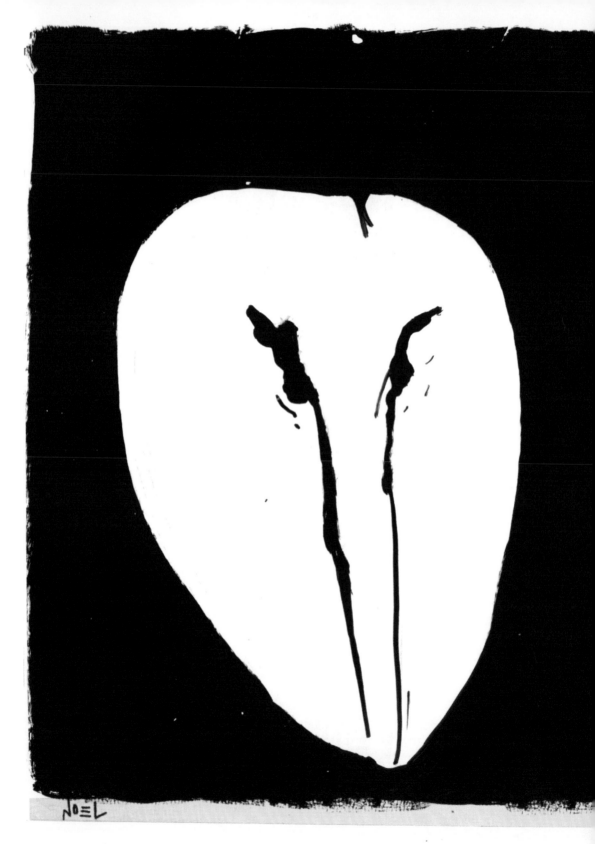

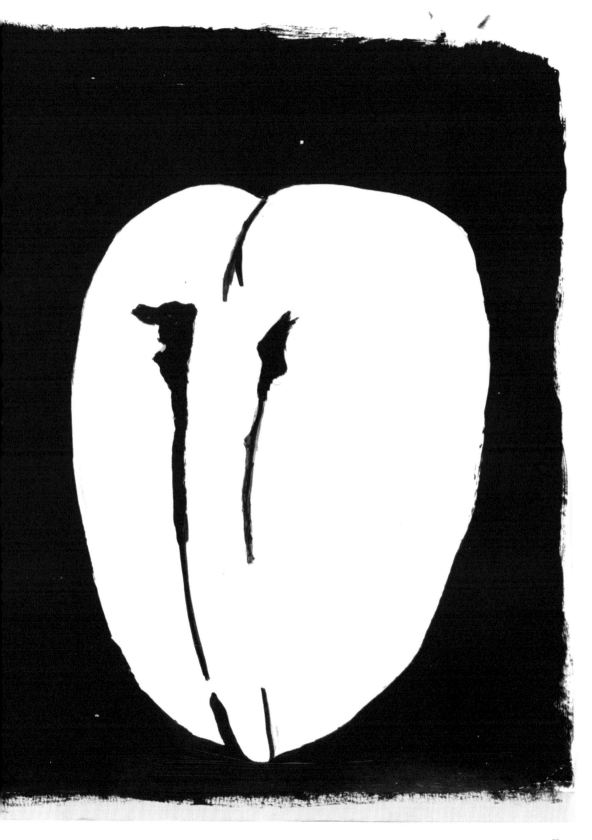

Noel

SELF PORTRAIT WITH FRIED
EGG FOR AN EYE.
(IN DA CHELSEA HOTEL)

charles

NOEL

The Guess Who Boys

Charles, Max, Robert and Richard

CHARLES

MAX

THE GUESS WHO BOYS   BASED ON A CONCEPT BY NOEL & DEE PLUME.

CHARLES WAS A BIT DOWN AFTER HE SPLIT UP WITH HIS GIRLFRIEND. MAX INVITED HIM OUT. MAX TOLD CHARLES THAT HE, RICHARD AND ROBERT (ALL RECENTLY DIVORCED) WENT OUT EVERY FRIDAY TO A LOCAL WINE BAR AFTER WORK TO HAVE A DRINK, RELAX AND MEET LADIES. DESPITE THE TEN YEAR AGE GAP BETWEEN CHARLES AND THE OTHERS HE WAS INTRIGUED AND AGREED TO TAG ALONG. MAX SHOUTED " THE THING ABOUT ME IS I JUST LOVE LIFE." CHARLES TRIED NOT TO LAUGH AT THIS OUTBURST AND WONDERED IF MAX'S HAIR WAS NATURALLY CURLY OR RECENTLY PERMED.

THE NEXT DAY MAX AND CHARLES ARRIVED AT THE BAR TOGETHER TO FIND ROBERT ALREADY THERE KNOCKING BACK THE WHISKY SOURS. ROBERT HADN'T SPOKEN SINCE HIS DIVORCE HAD COME THROUGH. HE ONLY ANSWERED QUESTIONS OCCASIONALLY BY SCRIBBLING ANSWERS ON TO A SMALL PAD HE KEPT IN THE TOP POCKET OF HIS SHIRT.

MAX SUGGESTED CHAMPAGNE AND AS THE BAR MAN OPENED THE BOTTLE THE CORK FLEW ACROSS THE ROOM HITTING RICHARD STRAIGHT BETWEEN THE EYES AS HE ENTERED THE BAR. RICHARD, A NERVOUS CHARACTER AT THE BEST OF TIMES, ~~DIVED UNDER THE BAR~~ THOUGHT HE HAD BEEN SHOT AND DIVED UNDER THE BAR, COVERING HIMSELF IN LADIES' HAND BAGS.

TWO HOURS LATER ROBERT WAS SITTING ON THE MIDDLE OF THE DANCE FLOOR WITH HIS SHOES AND SOCKS OFF SCRIBBLING THE WORDS "NO" INTO HIS SMALL NOTE PAD OVER AND OVER AGAIN.

MAX WAS OVER THE OTHER SIDE OF THE CLUB SHARING A BOOTH WITH THREE HANDSOME OLDER LADIES. CHARLES COULD OCCASIONALLY HEAR HIM BANGING THE TABLE AND SHOUTING " THE THING ABOUT ME IS I JUST LOVE LIFE."

RICHARD WAS EXPLAINING TO CHARLES IN DETAIL THAT SINCE HIS DIVORCE HE HADN'T HAD A SINGLE DATE AND THAT THE LADIES HE MET SEEMED PUT OFF BY HIS JOB AS AN ACCOUNTANT AND THAT HE WAS GOING TO START SAYING HE WAS A SPY INSTEAD. HE ASKED CHARLES IF HE THOUGHT HE COULD PASS HIMSELF OFF AS A SPY BUT CHARLES COULDN'T CONCENTRATE ON WHAT RICHARD WAS SAYING BECAUSE THE LUMP ON HIS HEAD FROM THE CHAMPAGNE CORK NOW RESEMBLED ONE OF THOSE BLUNT HORNS ON A GIRAFFE'S HEAD. AS RICHARD TALKED ENDLESSLY ABOUT BEING A SPY CHARLES DESPERATELY TRIED TO STOP HIMSELF TAKING OFF HIS COAT AND HANGING IT ON RICHARD'S LUMP.

HE WONDERED IF YOU COULD HANG A COAT ON RICHARD'S LUMP. HE THOUGHT THAT A WINDCHEATER WOULD BE EASY. BUT A WET SHEEPSKIN WOULD BE TOO HEAVY. HE FANTASIZED ABOUT HANGING COATS OF DIFFERENT WEIGHTS AND SIZES ON RICHARD'S LUMP.

WHEN CHARLES CAME TO HE HAD NO IDEA HOW MUCH TIME HE HAD SPENT IN HIS HUMAN COAT HOOK DAY DREAM.

ROBERT HAD BEEN THROWN OUT FOR SPITTING. MAX HAD LEFT WITH THREE OF A POSSIBLE FOUR LADIES HE HAD BEEN ENTERTAINING. SO CHARLES AGREED TO SHARE A CAB HOME WITH RICHARD.
IT WASN'T UNTIL CHARLES GOT OUT THE CAB THAT HE REALISED RICHARD LIVED OVER THE OTHER SIDE OF THE GUESS WHO BOARD AND HAD ONLY AGREED TO SHARE A CAB SO HE COULD TALK FOR A FURTHER TWENTY MINUTES ABOUT BEING A SPY.

IT WAS THE LAST TIME CHARLES EVER WENT OUT WITH RICHARD, ROBERT OR MAX AGAIN.

THOSE BOYS WERE TOTAL DICK HEADS.

ROBERT

RICHARD

BLACK JACK

CROCODILE DREAMS

I DREAMED I WAS ON HOLIDAY
AND A CROCODILE WAS IN MY
BATHROOM WEARING MY CONVERSE
TRAINERS. I PUSHED HIM INTO THE
BATH AND THE WATER WAS BOILING
AND HIS SKIN CAME OFF.

I NEVER FELT SO BAD.

HE RAN OUT ~~OUT~~ OF THE SPANISH VILLA
AND THAT NIGHT I COULD STILL HEAR HIM
SCREAMING IN THE DISTANCE.

WHISTLING LIKE A KETTLE.

HOLLERING IN CROCODILLIAN AGONY.

ONE OF HIS KNEES WAS HEAVILY
STRAPPED AND HE HAD A TUPPER WARE
CONTAINER FULL OF NADAL'S SWEATBANDS.

MOD WOLF!

HOWLING AT THE MOD

PAUL WELLAWOLF

TARGET MOON.

LOVE IS ....

TWO WALNUTS LOOKING
INTO THE MIDDLE DISTANCE
ILLUMINATED BY THE MOON
LARGE AND HUGE
LIKE AN ALABASTER
DISH

DABOKI THE
DISH LICKER
EATS RAGS AND
SCRAPS OF LEATHER
AND RUNS OFF INTO
THE NIGHT
CACKLING AND
DANCING

RICHARD PRYOR DOING AN IMPRESSION
OF DALEY THOMPSON.

TONY " MMMM CREAMY."
MORPH " SIMPLY RACIST."

52

Noel 99

KEV ON THE PIPES

54

BUBBLE GUM CATS

NOEL

Noehr

ABSOLUTELY

NO BANANAS

ABSOLUTELY

NO BANANAS

64

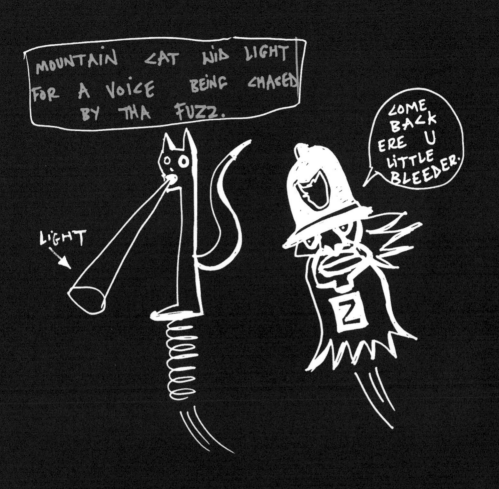

BBC THREE

I WAS IN FRANCE WHEN JULIAN CALLED ME TO
LET ME KNOW BBC THREE HAD OFFERED US
A PILOT EPISODE OF THE MIGHTY BOOSH.
I HAD TO WALK OUT INTO THE MIDDLE OF
A FIELD TO GET A SIGNAL ON MY PHONE.
~~(THANKS ORANGE YOU BOLL BAGS)~~
AFTER HEARING THE NEWS I JUMPED UP AND
DOWN AND NOTICED A COW ~~~~ IN THE
NEXT FIELD LOOKING AT ME. ~~I SAID TO~~
~~IT "I HAVE JUST GOT A PILOT." AND~~
~~WALKED BACK TO THE HOUSE. AS I~~

AS I WAS WALKING BACK TO THE HOUSE I'M SURE
I HEARD THE COW SAY " IT WON'T GO TO A
                                           SERIES."

MEDUSA AS PAGE 3 GIRL

PRINCE DI SHOOVNA →

FIGO THE FRUIT FLY
AND
RAYMOND BOOMBOX
AND
THE GASH A
FIRST ~~CLASS~~ CLASS
SICKO

STRIP SEARCH

BUM BUM TIMES

I DID THIS PAINTING AFTER I WAS HAND
CUFFED AND STRIP SEARCHED BY THE
POLICE FOR NO REASON AT ALL. ALSO
AS I LAY FACE DOWN ON THE PAVEMENT
WAITING FOR A VAN. SOME ONE FILMED
ME FROM A BUS AND SOLD IT TO THE
NEWS OF THE WORLD. ONE OF THE
WORST SUNDAYS EVER!
THIS PAINTING IS DEDICATED TO THE
DEDICATED MEMBERS OF THE FORCE WHO
LOOKED UP MY BUM BUM AND THE
LOVELY MAN WHO SOLD THE PHOTOS TO
THE PAPERS. A CHARMING MAN WHO
I WOULD LIKE TO GET TO KNOW
BETTER. ITS A RUMOUR THAT I
WANT TO PUT MY HIGH HEEL BOOT
IN HIS EYE AND TWIST IT.

BEAUTIFUL INDIAN WOMEN AT THE ZOO

princess di shoovna

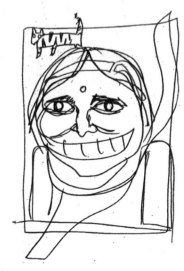

NOEL

83

THE TREES HAVE SECRETS

60s Syd

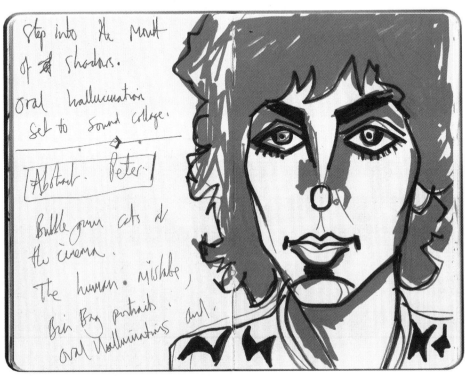

Step into the Mouth
of the shadows.

Oral hallucination
set to sound collage.

Abstract. Peter.

Bubble gum cats at
the cinema.

The human mistake,
Bean Bag portraits.
Oral hallucinations and.

JAFFA CAKES.

THIS PAINTING HAD JAFFA
CAKES FOR EYES. BUT IN
THE HOT AFTERNOON SUN
THEY MELTED OFF!
 LEAVING STICKY WHITE
 ~~SEE~~ SPHERES IN THEIR PLACE.

I LIKED THE EFFECT. ~~●~~
 ~~SEE~~ LATER THAT DAY
AN ANNOYING WOMAN
BARGED INTO MY STUDIO
TRYING TO SELL ME HER
HOME MADE CURRY. SHE
WOULD NOT STOP TALKING.
AT ONE POINT SHE HELPED
 HERSELF TO ONE OF THE
 FALLEN JAFFA CAKES. I
VIEWED HER AND SAID NOTHING
OF THE SUPER GLUE I HAD USED
 ~~EARLIER~~ TO STICK ~~●~~ IT TO
TO THE PAINTING EARLIER THAT
 MORNING.

THE SNITCH

THE ARGUMENT.

"LOOK EVERYONE, IT'S SLOW MOTION COOPER."
"QUICK, SPRAY HIM, CHILDREN.
HE'S GETTING AWAY!"

HAPPY BIRTHDAY RADIANT CHILD

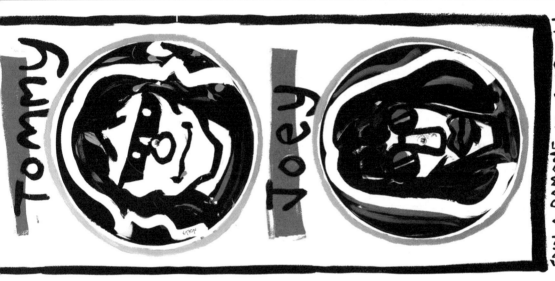

THE INCIDENT

THE TWO DUBIOUS CHARACTERS AT THE SIDE OF THE ROAD
SAW IT HAPPEN.

THE BUGS CHASING EACHOTHER ROUND THE LAMP POST
SAW IT HAPPEN.

THE DARK FIGURE HANGING FROM THE TREE SAW IT HAPPEN.

THE SPINNING WHEEL ON THE ~~BICY~~ DISCARDED BICYCLE SAW
IT HAPPEN.

THE ALBINO CHILD AT THE WINDOW SAW IT HAPPEN.

THE BIG BLACK BIRD ON THE ROOF OF THE TRUCK SAW
IT HAPPEN.

THE BEARS WALKING IN SINGLE FILE SAW IT HAPPEN.

THE APE FORCED TO DRESS AS A WIZARD SAW IT HAPPEN.

WHAT THEY HAD SEEN WAS SO UNUSUAL THEY ALL AGREED
NEVER TO SPEAK OF IT AGAIN.

BUT THEY MET ONCE A YEAR TO MAKE SURE IT HAD
REMAINED A SECRET FROM THE WORLD.

THEY WOULD GET DRUNK AT THESE MEETINGS
AND SOMETIMES HOLD HANDS AND WEEP.

THE STRANGENESS OF WHAT THEY HAD SEEN HAD
MANACLED THEM TOGETHER.

THEY WERE FAMILY NOW.

~~THEIR~~ THEIR MEETINGS BECAME MORE REGULAR AND
FOR A WHILE THEY DID EVERYTHING TOGETHER.

THEN SUDDENLY ONE DAY WITH NO WARNING THEY
ALL CLIMBED INTO A BOAT, ROWED OUT INTO THE MIDDLE
OF THE OCEAN AND COMMITTED SUICIDE.

Nosl

Noel 08

FRIDGE DOOR LEANING AGAINST THE PEBBLE
DASHED BUNGALOW. ARTIFICIAL LIGHT, THE STILLNESS
OF THE NIGHT. RED FOX LOOKING BACK AT YOU.
SADDLES FASHIONED FROM D.V.D MENUS.
WALLOPING FRUIT SALAD, BURNING ~~~~ HOUMOUS.
ORCHESTRAL STRINGS AND THE PURPLE SHAPE
THAT REPRESENTS MILKSHAKES.
RODS AND CONES MORE VISIBLE THAN THE
LANDSCAPE. DUSTBIN LID CRASHES DOWN ON
YOUR BACKBONE. ~~~~~~~~~~~~~~~~
PANTS IN THE SKIP.
VAGUE MEMORY.
PURPLE SHAPE THE PROVIDER .
OF SOFT WHITE MEAT

                    FOR THE SEX
                        INDUSTRY.

TANIA WADE - MY HOOLIGAN
ART DEALER!. A BLOND BOMBSHELL
AND A SOHO ANGEL.

(Black skull)

drown in lumpy red silk.

Black ~~beads~~ and blue beads
Embedded deep into soft bread Faces

Laughing. gagging skulls with
rotten poles dancing and
Clicking in the night.

117

The Tale of the Tiger Spider

THERE WAS ONCE A SMALL VILLAGE IN THE SOUTH OF
FRANCE FAMOUS FOR INHABITING REAMS OF LEMON
YELLOW BUTTERFLIES. THE MAGICAL CREATURES WERE A
HUGE TOURIST ATTRACTION AND MADE THE VILLAGE
WEALTHY AND VIBRATE WITH ~~HAPPYNESS~~ HAPPYNESS AND
BEAUTY.   ONE DAY COMPLETELY UNANNOUNCED A
STRANGE BEAST CALLED THE ~~TIGE~~ TIGER SPIDER
TURNED UP IN THE FOREST ON THE EDGE OF TOWN.
THE TIGER SPIDER ATTRACTED THE BUTTERFLIES AND
SPENT THE WARM AFTERNOONS DANCING WITH THEM.
AS IF IN A TRANCE OR A FRENZY.
THE VILLAGERS WERE ~~SO~~ SUSPICIOUS OF THE STRANGE
CREATURE AND THOUGHT HE WOULD HARM THEIR PRECIOUS
LEMON YELLOW INSECTS. OR POSSIBLY MUNCH THEM DOWN
FOR FOOD. THEY CALLED A MEETING AND DECIDED TO TAKE
ACTION. LOCKING UP THE TIGER SPIDER IN THE VILLAGE PRISON.
WITHIN HOURS OF THIS HAPPENING THE BUTTERFLIES FLED THE
VILLAGE NEVER TO BE SEEN AGAIN. AS A RESULT OF THIS
THE VILLAGE SOON BECAME DESOLATE AND POOR.
THE TIGER SPIDER SPENT HIS FINAL YEARS IN PAIN FOR HE
WAS DEEPLY IN LOVE WITH THE BUTTERFLIES. THEY WERE IN FACT
HIS WIVES. HE DIED OF A BROKEN HEART BUT NOT BEFORE
SCRATCHING OUT A LOVE SONNET TO HIS INSECT WIVES ON THE
PRISON WALL.
THE VILLAGERS FELT SO GUILTY AND MOVED BY THE
LOVE SONNET THEY DECIDED TO KNOCK DOWN
THE PRISON AND USE THE LAST OF THEIR MONEY
TO BUILD A CHAPEL IN ITS PLACE IN HONOUR
OF THE TIGER SPIDER WHO HAD DIED OF A
BROKEN HEART.

THE CHAPEL⬛ WAS DECORATED WITH LEMON
YELLOW BUTTERFLIES AND LINE DRAWINGS OF THE
TIGER SPIDER DANCING WITH HIS TINY WINES.
(AS IF IN A FRENZY OR A TRANCE.)
THE CHAPEL BECAME FAMOUS THROUGHOUT THE
WORLD. THE PLACE TO VISIT FOR PEOPLE WITH
BROKEN HEARTS. THE BROKEN HEARTED
WOULD COMFORT EACH OTHER AND FEEL A SENSE
OF HOPE SITTING IN THE CHAPEL AMONGST
THE LEMON YELLOW BUTTERFLIES.
ITS POPULARITY SAVED THE VILLAGE
GENERATING WEALTH AND THE BUZZ OF HAPPINESS
AND BEAUTY ONCE MORE.
IN TIME THE LEMON YELLOW BUTTERFLIES
RETURNED AND SURROUNDED THE GREAT CHAPEL
LIKE A GOLDEN MIST. OFTEN MAKING
PATTERNS IN THE SKY AND OCCASIONALLY FORMING
TO CREATE THE IMAGE OF THE TIGER SPIDER
DANCING (AS IF IN A FRENZY OR A TRANCE.)

KIM DRAGGED THE HUGE CHINESE SHARK UP THREE FLIGHTS OF STAIRS INTO THE EGYPTIAN PALACE. IT WAS STILL BREATHING AS HE SMASHED ITS HEAD IN WITH A CHELSEA BOOT. "TYPICAL OF YOU." JASON BARKED. "YOUR VOICE IS A RACING CAR." "YUM YUM TIMES". KIM MUMBLED LAUGHING TO HIMSELF AND TURNING AWAY. "THAT'S A HAMMERHEAD SHARK" SAID JASON, HITTING THE ~~CREATURE WITH A~~ HAMMERHEAD WITH A HAMMER. THE ~~SEA~~ BONES INSIDE THE THICK RUBBER SKIN STARTED TO BREAK INTO SMALL PIECES UNTIL THE SHARK BECAME A LONG GREY BAG FULL OF JUNK BALLS. BONEY PUZZLE PIECES SLOSHING AROUND INSIDE THE BLUE SLEEPING BAG WITH FINS. THE EYES WERE STILL WORKING AND SHIFTED IN THEIR SOCKETS FROM MY FACE TO JASON'S AS IF WATCHING AN EXCITING TENNIS MATCH. THE SHARK DIDN'T EXIST AND ~~NEITHER~~ NEITHER DID I NOR JASON.

JIM MORRISON

WE ATE ~~xxxxxxx~~ FROM THE
EDGES INTO THE MIDDLE. WHEN OUR
NOSES WERE TOUCHING WE KNEW WE HAD
EATEN ENOUGH. WE SAT UP IN LAUREL
CANYON WAITING FOR THE FUCKER
TO KICK IN. THE CITY OF ANGELS
SPREAD OUT BELOW US LIKE A
SEA OF BLINKING YELLOW EYES.
I TURNED TO JIM AND SAID
"I FEEL SLIGHTLY UNUSUAL."
JIM WAS EATING A CAMPER VAN
WITH HIS ~~xxxx~~ FINGER MOUTH.

I POURED A BUCKET of
FABULOUS RED WAR STORIES OVER
HIS TORSO AND HE POINTED TO
A CAT FLAP IN THE MOON.
WE SCURRIED INSIDE LIKE TWO
HUNGRY TABBY CATS. ONCE INSIDE
THE MOONS CHALKY WHITE FORM,
I WAS ABLE TO FLOAT AROUND
IN THE AIR LIKE A WEIGHTLESS
PIGS BLADDER.

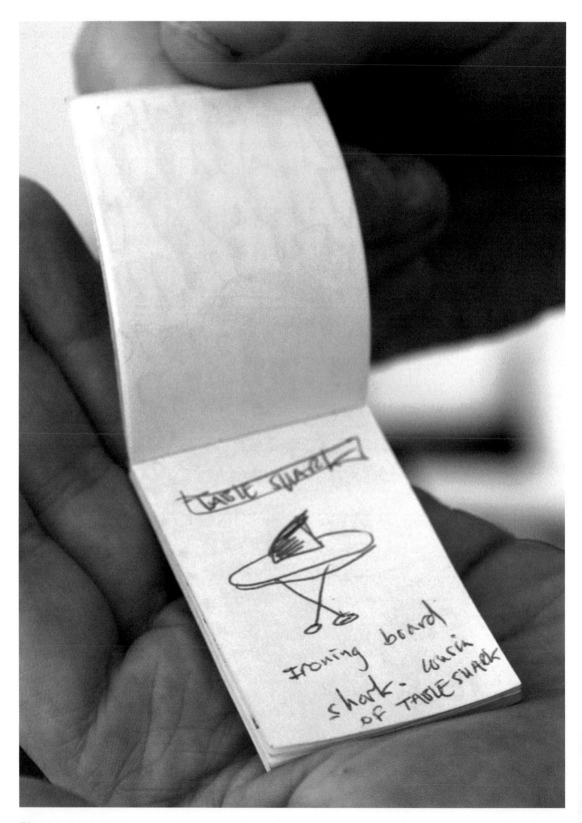

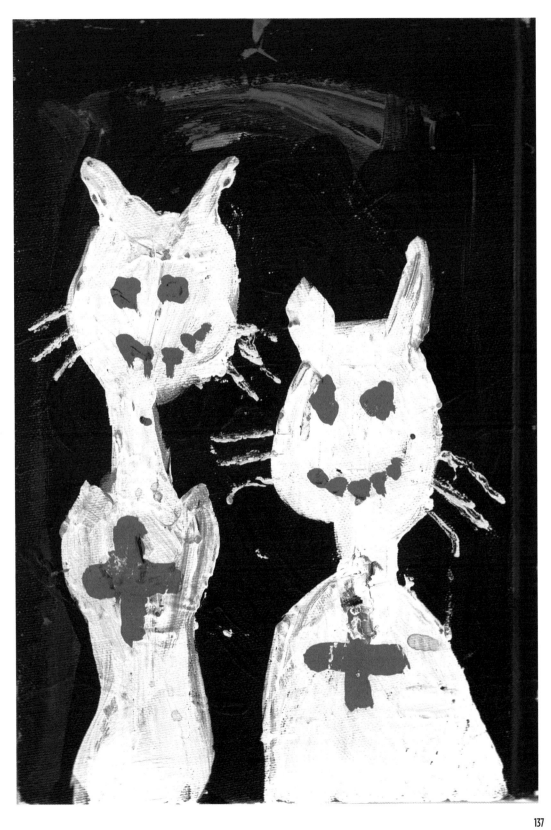

MY TINY CHILDREN X

A Flask of Liquid Elvis

ELVIS'S GRANDMOTHER DODGER AND TONY THE SMALL DOG FISH WHO LIVED ON HER WIDE COLLARS.

I ONLY MET ELVIS ABOUT 300 TIMES IN REAL LIFE BUT ~~I~~ OUR MEETINGS USUALLY FOLLOWED A SIMILAR PATTERN. HE WOULD ARRIVE IN THE MIDDLE OF THE NIGHT CARRYING A BAG OF HARD-BOILED EGGS. HE WOULD THEN PRODUCE ~~A CATAPULT~~ 2 CATAPULTS AND WE WOULD SPEND THE REST OF THE NIGHT FIRING EGGS INTO EACH OTHER'S FACES. THE LOSER WAS THE FIRST TO GIVE IN. ONE TIME ELVIS ~~USED~~ USED CONCRETE EGGS IN AN ATTEMPT TO CHEAT. BUT I HAD LINED ~~HAD~~ THE INSIDE OF MY FACE ~~LINED~~ WITH A THIN SHEET OF BRONZE THE WEEK BEFORE. ~~AS~~ AS THE CONCRETE EGGS EXPLODED ONE AFTER ~~THE~~ ANOTHER ON MY FACE ELVIS WENT GREEN AND BURPED UP A SMALL AMOUNT OF SICK IN TOTAL DISBELIEF.

ELVIS COULD TALK TO TIGERS BUT WAS SURPRISED TO FIND THEY ALL SOUNDED LIKE JOE PASQUALE.

ELVIS

ELVIS PHONED ME UP AND ASKED IF I WOULD TAKE SOME SCISSORS ACROSS THE ~~BORDER~~ BORDER FOR HIM. I AGREED. ~~████~~. TWO WEEKS LATER ELVIS FOUND ME IN WATERSTONES TALKING TO A SHOE WITH A FACE DRAWN ON IT. ~~████~~

DEFORMED ELVIS CRYING GAS.

A GAS TEARDROP.

The Island of Dr Gannis

I had always wanted to be on him 'Record Breakers'. As a child, Roy Castle and Norris McWhirter represented two icons of achievement to me. Roy, with his tap dancing shoes made from old trumpets, and Norris, with the longest memory in Europe, (which he coiled up and kept about his person like fireman's hose). It was my favourite TV show as a child and it had been my aim, ever since, to get in 'The Guinness Book of Records' as a man.

Which is why two years ago I set off from a lighthouse in Seaview on the Isle of Wight, inside the world's largest paper airplane. Inconceivably I managed to reach as far as the Indian Ocean before disaster struck. I was trying to take a Polaroid of myself mid-flight (as verification for Norris) when I somehow lost control of the craft. The plane began to splutter and vibrate and the nose pointed directly up into the air, heading straight for the sun. I could do nothing to stop it and a month and a half later the sun was so close and the heat so unbearable that I had no choice but to roll up my sleeves. I was now flying dangerously close to the Earth's fiery orb and knew in my heart that someone was going to pay the price for this act of insanity, and that someone was probably going to be me (as I was the only person on the plane). My co-pilot James Black had abandoned the ship earlier on (two minutes after take off). He mumbled something about it being too dangerous for someone with such good cheekbones and then skipped off towards the Groucho club. How he expected to gain entrance without my presence remains a mystery to me.

Five hours later I had not only rolled up my sleeves but had taken off my poncho and was using my travel iron to remove two large creases from it. The heat from the iron coupled with the fact I was now less than a metre away from the sun was making my top lip perspire slightly. I reached into a drawer in my cowboy hat and pulled out a packet of wet wipes. They smelt pure and fresh. I took one out and gently placed it over my skull to protect me from getting a tan. This was the last thing I remember doing (apart from making a fruit salad and reading five hundred emails). It was around this point that my teeth started to melt and I knew I was in big trouble. The plane caught fire and I jumped overboard using my poncho as a rudimentary parachute. I floated gently down to the turquoise ocean beneath me.

I had, like a modern day Icarus, flown too close to the sun and was paying the price. I knew people would see my actions as arrogant or vain. A man who lived his life with his head in the clouds. A man who wanted to be closer to God. The truth of it was I just wanted to see my name in 'The Guinness Book of Records'. I hit the water with a splash and emptied out my brown leather Doctor's bag, using it as a makeshift dinghy. I climbed inside and used my bank card as a paddle. The waves were too strong and I gave up paddling and just bobbed around for two and a half months with only food and water to survive on. One afternoon I was polishing off some orange and green the last when things took a turn for the worse. One of my gold fillings became dislodged and started to sink into the water below me. I made a grab for it, splashing around in the hot, green, salty water, and suddenly noticed I wasn't alone. Gliding underneath the boat were about a thousand sharks. They moved around gracefully like grey torpedos. Unfortunately my boat had alerted them to my presence. Within seconds they were on the attack. A huge shark maybe thirty foot long was heading straight towards me. I closed my eyes and had only a second to think about how much this attack would hurt. Suddenly everything went white and I saw the face of Steve Owen Bush in the sky above me.

Two hours later I woke up on the deck of a ship with two men staring down at me. One of them was a smartly dressed sailor, the other a kind of deformed cabin boy with whiskers, who seemed to resemble Elvis Presley. He made heavy breathing noises as he trundled about the vessel moving cages about. Cages containing a huge array of exotic animals. Red pandas, bears and penguins along with a Labrador and a wallaby (both called Martin Thompson). The animals seemed content in their tiny prisons. Or drugged perhaps. It transpired that the two men had rescued me from the sharks, hoisting me out of the water with one of those long poles shop keepers use in Camden market to retrieve expensive jackets usually not for sale, up in the rafters of their retro kingdoms. The captain explained to me that I would have to travel to a nearby island with them and wait for a bigger ship to pass by that could take me back to England. He offered me some diet Coke and a handful of carrots. I munched down the goods and quickly regained my strength. I felt safe aboard the ship, apart from the presence of Mungo the cabin boy, who avoided eye contact at all costs and looked as though he might erupt into violence at any given moment. The captain often shouted at Mungo and beat him with a bamboo cane. The poor brute had a sadness in his eyes that chilled me to the bone.

We finally reached the island and Mungo remained on the boat, shifting crates around with the strength of ten men. The captain and I headed across the white beach towards the dense jungle of this tropical paradise. Once inside the botanical forest I saw strange blue flowers the size of dustbin lids. Flowers that seemed to dance and move about in the breeze. Flowers that seemed to turn to face you as you walked by. There were also gangs of small bright red ponies the size of cats that leapt across giant lily pads in a purple spotted lake. This was a strange and beautiful island. Frightening and yet soothing. You couldn't help but become intoxicated by the amount of nature. It almost engulfed you.

"I will show you to your room before it gets too dark," the captain mumbled. Before us was a large white building that looked like a Moroccan palace, impeccably tended to in every way. Luxurious gardens surrounded the palace and sprinklers could be heard gushing out water onto the pretty flowers that seemed to grow everywhere. As we approached two doors in the side of the building the captain seemed bothered by something and quickly guided me into the door on the left.

"Your room is in here," he barked at me.

"What's in this door?" I asked pointing to the door on the right.

"The Doctor is in there! We must not disturb him while he is working."

"The Doctor?" I enquired.

"Yes, Dr Gannis. This is his house."

The captain now seemed furious with me and pulled me through the door on the left and up two flights of stairs into a large comfortable room, decked out with a four-poster bed and and a small writing desk.

"Get some rest now and I will see you in the morning. I have to go and unload the boat before nightfall."

The captain had gained his composure and was back to his charming self.

"What are the animals for?" I asked, pushing my luck.

"Dr Gannis uses them in his work. Now no more questions, it's late!"

With this the captain turned and left the room. Much to my horror I heard the door lock behind him. I ran to it and violently grabbed the handle. Sure enough I had been locked in my room. But why? I ran to the window and opened the purple wooden shutters. My heart began to race. The window had thick iron bars

across it. I was trapped. All manner of thoughts consumed me. Why had I been brought here and why was I being held prisoner in my own room? The image of Mungo flashed into my mind over and over again like a deformed siren. I felt dizzy and passed out, still weak and malnourished from my ordeal.

I awoke a few minutes before midnight in complete darkness. From my window I could hear the screams of someone or something, howling in agony. Screams that seemed to be creating the tune of 'Jail House Rock'. The sounds were like nothing I had ever experienced before and almost made me throw up. I had to get out of this place. I opened the shutters to my window, letting in a whole crate of moonlight. Now able to see, I skilfully picked the lock on the door with the pin from my Kiss badge. As the door swung open I froze, not knowing who or what to expect. The hallway was dark and silent as I tip-toed down the corridor and climbed through a small window into the garden below. My first thoughts were to start running and never turn back, then try and take control of the small boat I had arrived on and make my escape. But the sounds would not allow me to leave. Something was being tortured or mutilated inside the room next to mine and I had to know what it was. I crept up to the steel door marked 'Laboratory' and pushed it open. I walked inside and was confronted by a long thin room. The walls were lined with cages and cages of screaming animals, all witness to some kind of horror taking place at the other end of the room. My legs moved me along like a clockwork toy, closer and closer to the horror. At first I thought some strange ritual or sacrifice was taking place.

As I got close enough to see I froze, bathed in absolute fear and disgust. Before me was a sight now embedded into my mind. There was an operating table in front of me and a creature writhing around on it covered in blood and bodily fluids. Leaning over this shrieking homunculus was Dr Gannis, stitching and cutting intensely, as if trying to save the poor wretch's life. Next to the doctor was an assistant, passing one tool after another to the doctor with an hideously deformed animal claw. I gagged and stumbled backwards, upsetting a cage full of golden Tamarin monkeys. The doctor, his assistant, and the thing on the operating table all looked over at me. Everything fell silent. I could not speak and moved around the floor like a deranged insect. The assistant pulled down his green surgical mask and revealed his face. It was the face of a leopard that somehow resembled Elvis Presley, the King of Rock n Roll...a deformed hybrid with a chicken's body, wearing satin trousers and Chelsea boots. The creature shuffled about from one leg to the other and made a deep sound like a coffee machine. The figure had the same air of deformity as Mungo the cabin boy and like Mungo resembled Elvis Presley. The creature on the table was even more disturbing. It seemed to have a pig's body and a donkey's head with a black quiff and sideburns. The creature was dressed as Elvis during his Vegas years and its top lip seemed to move independently from the rest of its face, up and down producing a kind of sexy, grotesque Elvis pout. As I pulled myself up onto my feet a group of five or more shadowy figures appeared from the back of the room and lurched towards me - all as disgusting as the creature on the table, all resembling Elvis in some kind of monstrous way. Dr Gannis calmly instructed these abominations to "capture me" and I ran for my life.

The next five minutes were a blur. I stumbled through bracken, fell into a stream and hit my head on several large rocks. Finally I fought my way through the undergrowth to the beach and could see the boat bobbing up and down gently on the water. The angry pack of Elvis mutants behind me were carrying torches and making horrible noises and singing 'Hound Dog'. They were gaining on me all the time. I sprinted across the moonlit sand and waded head first into the sea. What would they do to me? I wondered. Would they take me back to Dr Gannis as instructed? Or just tear me limb from limb in an animalistic frenzy? I climbed up the side of the boat and onto the deck, pulled up the anchor and turned on the engine, steering the boat away from the mangled pack of horror slabs below me. A mandrill Elvis scurried up the side of the boat and I smashed him back down with an oar. I had made it. I had escaped from this living carnival of fiends. I turned to take control of the wheel once more, and there he was. Mungo the sable boy. He was playing a guitar and gyrating his hips. He dropped the guitar and struck me on the side of the head, knocking me down with one blow. The next thing I remember was being lifted like a rag doll above Mungo's head and thrown back over the side of the boat to the grasping mutilated gang below.

I awoke six weeks later to find that my bandages were being removed by a wolf nurse with Elvis side burns. The light hurt my eyes and my face felt swollen. I looked down, and to my horror I had the hard shell-like body of some kind of crustacean. I was a giant crab with six legs poked into tight black leather Elvis collars from his '68 Comeback Special'. I also felt like I had some kind of trunk or beak but there was no way of telling. My eyesight was poor and my ability to think had been largely eradicated. The next thing I remember I was walking across the hot sand sideways, mumbling,

"Thank you very much."

I could feel the presence of others with me. There was an Elvis pony and a giraffe with a quiff wearing a diamante cape. These were my brothers and I knew we were family. But as the weeks passed by my gums began to bleed constantly and my genitals started to drag behind me, brushing against the jagged sand. I could now only see out of one eye and had a kind of asthma that made me dizzy and pass out several times a day. Occasionally I would have vague recollections of being on stage performing comedy. Other times I dreamed about a man with small eyes and a moustache but my head could not join the dots or make sense of these insane notions.

And so I lived out the rest of my life on the strange island of Dr Gannis, with my mutant Elvis friends. I never did find out why Dr Gannis was cutting up animals and fusing them with the DNA of Elvis Presley. Or why he had chosen me for one of his horrific experiments. Then one day my body grew cold and my legs started to crumble and I could no longer digest solid food. I sat on a big grey rock and looked out at the sea, waiting to die. For a split second Phil Jupitus flashed into my brain. I had no idea why. Or who Phil Jupitus was. A few moments later Alsatian Elvis sat next to me and licked my face. It was at this moment that I spotted a neighbouring island that I had never seen before. I contemplated the roll of fate and wondered what would have happened to me if I had been taken to this island instead. What's on that island? I thought. But I must have been thinking aloud, talking to myself, because Alsatian Elvis turned to me and said,

"That's the island of mutant Eddie Cochrans."

The End.

THE PARK KEEPER ARRIVED WEARING A SQUIRREL SKIN ~~GLUED~~ GLUED TO HIS FACE AND A TOP HAT. HE PRODUCED A MACHINE GUN FROM THE TRUNK OF HIS JEEP AND FIRED PEANUTS ~~AT~~ AT US FROM ~~SO~~ CLOSE RANGE. ELVIS SLOWED TIME DOWN AND WE CASUALLY WALKED OFF - HELPING OURSELVES TO THE OCCASIONAL PEANUT HANGING IN THE AIR. HOW COOL IS ELVIS I REMEMBER THINKING AS I ~~S~~ FELL INTO A DITCH.

ELVIS LETTING OUT A TOMMY SQEEKER.

ELVIS IN THE WINDOW

ELVIS LOOKED SO BEAUTIFUL IN THE GOLDEN SUIT OF ARMOUR I HAD GOTTEN HIM FOR HIS 40th BIRTHDAY.

ELVIS ~~DANCED~~ DANCED INTO THE GARDEN WEARING A FROG MASK. THE LIGHT MADE THE POND LOOK LIKE A MAGIC CRYSTAL BATH. A GIRL WALKED PAST EATING A DEAD CROW AND THE MOMENT WAS SPOILT.

ELVIS DID NOT CRY
VERY OFTEN BUT
WHEN HE DID
HE REALLY
WENT FOR IT.

THE
ELVIS
HOOF

ELVIS

ELVIS AND I SKIPPED TO THE
PARK HOLDING HANDS. ~~THE LAST~~
~~SOME . THE FOUR~~ IT WAS
CONKER SEASON. TWO SMALL BOYS
HAD FILLED A TESCO BAG ~~FULL~~ TO
THE BRIM WITH CHEESE CUTTERS AND
WERE HIGH UP IN THE BRANCHES OF
A TREE EXTRACTING MORE. ~~WE CUT THE~~
ELVIS AND I HELPED OURSELVES TO ~~THE~~
THEIR STASH AND ~~WE DID~~ THEN DID
~~THE~~ A WEE ON THEIR BIKES.

I TAPPED ELVIS'S QUIFF. IT WAS SOLID
BUT ALSO HOLLOW. "LISTEN." ELVIS
MUMBLED. FROM INSIDE THE BLACK
QUIFF YOU COULD ~~B~~ HEAR THE
NOISE OF A DISTANT CHILDRENS
PLAYGROUND.

ELVIS LIKED LOTS OF DIFFERENT TYPES OF MUSIC. HE ONCE TOLD ME HE PARTICULARLY LIKED 'TANGERINE DREAM'. HE TOLD ME THAT 'TANGERINE DREAM' ~~LIVED HERE~~ INSIDE HIS RADIATORS IN THE FORM OF A COMPLEX ICE MONSTER.

I'm not talking
to you any more

The Story of Peter Douglas.
HOOF CHAOS IN TOULON

ROBOT WAS NO MATCH FOR PETER.

Sorry guys

Hooves pummelling Iron vigilante with cool ease.

AND this is why

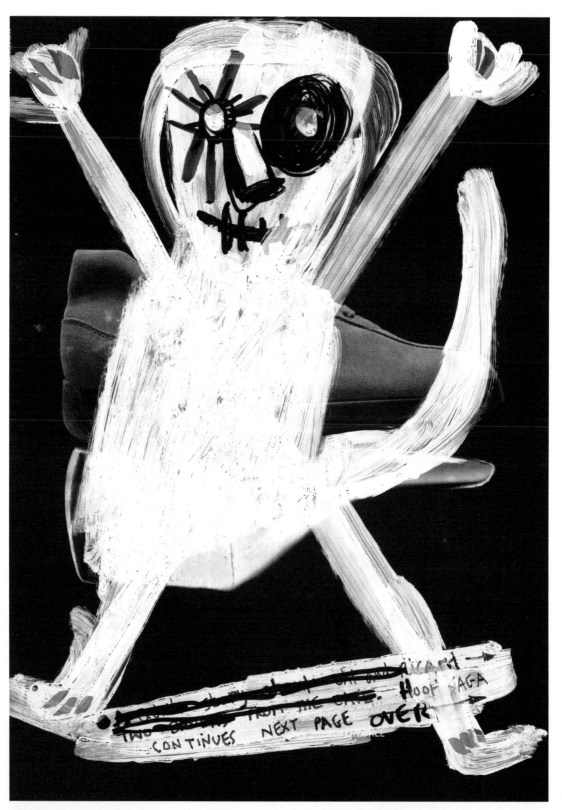

chi and Recard, outlaws wanted in 50 different states, ordered some vanilla tea, and some milk, for their Husky. The waiter was playing his little games, laughing at their outragious neon blue ponchos. chi told Recard to keep his cross eyed cool and dissapeared to use the toilet. The DOG PIG waiter returned spilling hot tea onto Alfies paws. Recard reached for his Gun in a flash chi entered with the body of a serpant destroying the waiter with lazers from da eyes.

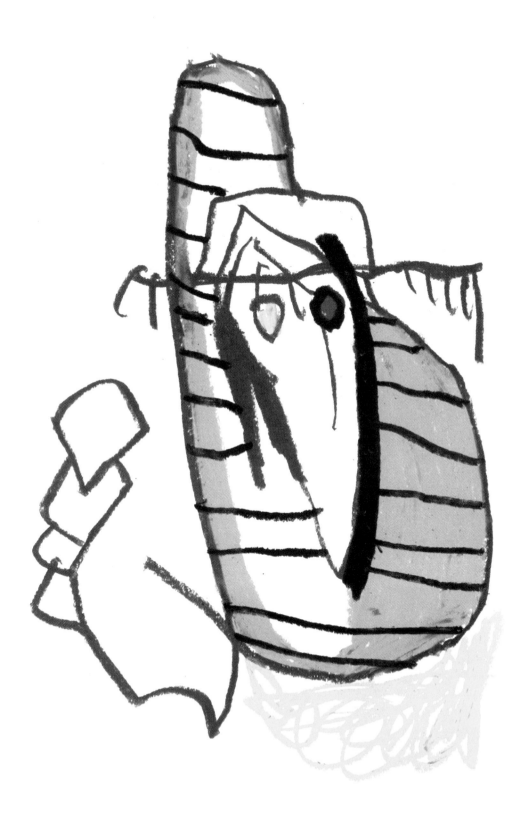

NOEL: OH LOOK AT ME I'M HAVING A LITTLE ART SHOW IN THE CAKE SHOP. PLEASE COME WON'T YOU?

TEX: I WILL BUT ONLY TO ▮SMASH YOUR FACE IN WITH MY SHOE.

NOEL: FINE I JUST NEED NUMBERS.

Psychedelic Jungle Book

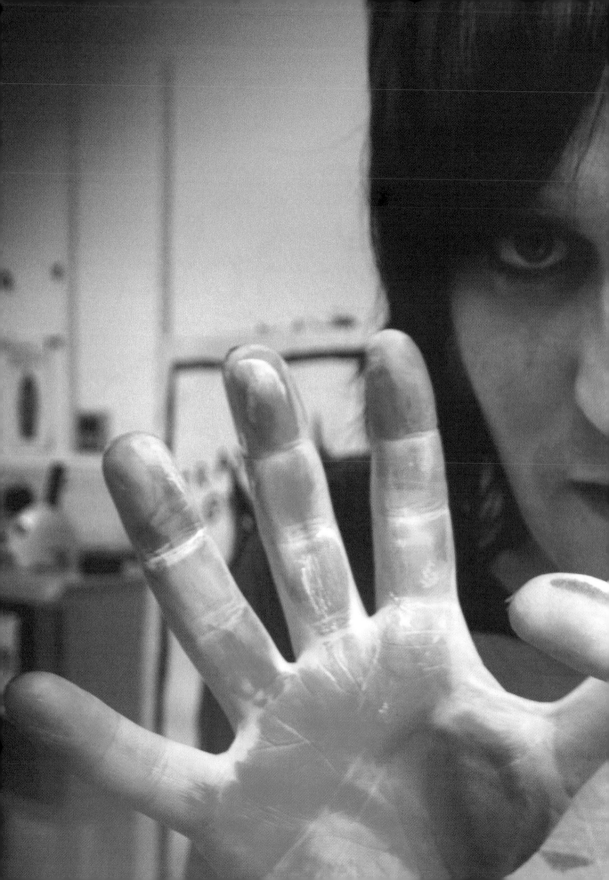

THE HUMAN MISTAKE
BEHIND
NIGEL COAN

Parvenu

GREAT DOUBLE ACTS

(TWO MINDS WORKING AS ONE.)
CHAZ N DAVE
HOPPER N FONDA
THOSE BLOKES OFF MASTER CHEF
JAMIE N HIS TORCH
FULL STOP N LITTLE COMMA.

The greek ~~~~ guy opposite me has no arms and a tight cylindrical ~~~~ Body Sausage apron ~~~~ Value, instead of a T-shirt.

214

rown AT once♥

215

Noel

NOEL

GHOST RIDER

WATER GHOSTS - GHOST RIDER

Fabric missiles

Japanese Royalty

idea

leaving a shadow an aura an
Impression of where they once were.

old gliders
chunky coy people
heavy boats
dipped in wet neat
colour.

Trail backs. / Blaze

COY

phantom fins   Ghost fins - delicate fabric.

kites — water kites   Soft   So old

You are only ever painting where they once were.

Always a few seconds behind

history of their movements. patterns of things →

← long since gone.   smooth Rainbow coloured
                        phantoms.

                        that can't be caught

stars of the   under
               water stars ✦
               under water shooting stars.

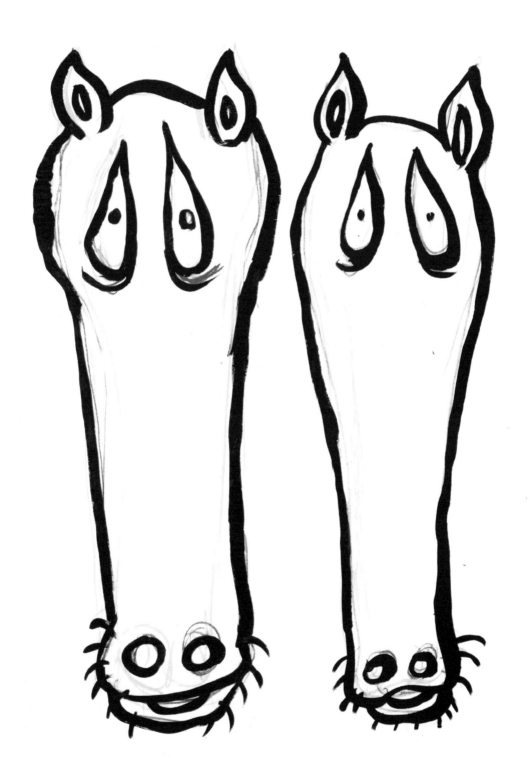

NOEL

228

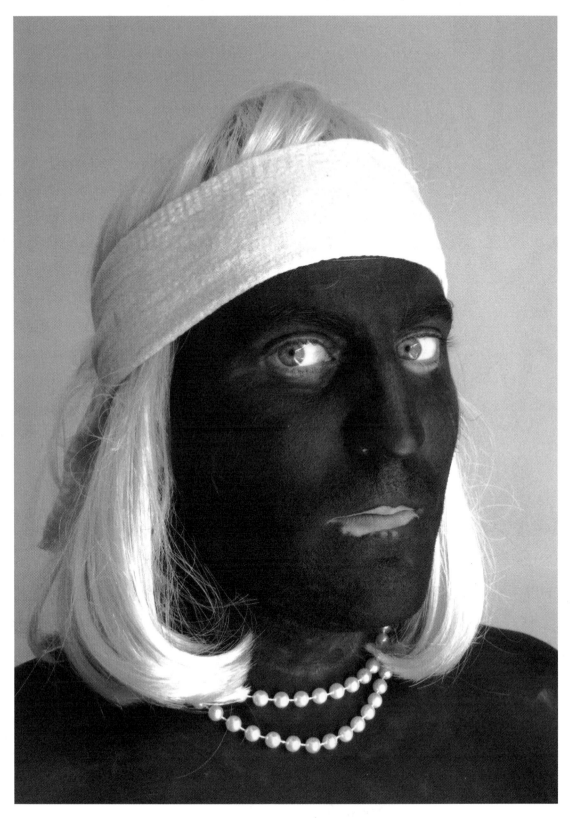

234

Bryan Ferry vs The Jelly Fox

BRYAN SUGGESTED WE SET UP AN
EGG AND SPOON RACE.
BRYAN FERRY WAS SO FAST AND WON EASILY.
ALTHOUGH LATER ON THAT DAY WHEN WE WERE
GETTING SOME TOAST I NOTICED BRYAN'S
EGG HAD BEEN HARD BOILED AND NAILED
TO THE SPOON WITH A GRAVITY PIN.

BRYAN'S BOWTIE DOUBLED UP AS A VAMPIRE BAT AND DURING THE RACE BECAME ENTANGLED IN MY HAIR. I FELT THE BOWTIE BAT BITE INTO MY HEAD AND ACTUALLY TEAR OFF A PORTION OF MY SCALP. AS I WAS RUNNING ALL I COULD THINK WAS RABIES, LOCK JAW, GREEN DEATH. THESE THOUGHTS MADE MY RUNNING STYLE JERKY AND MONSTER-LIKE.
BRYAN TAUNTED ME ~~LAUGHING~~ LAUGHING AND SAYING
" HA HA HA YOU RUN AS IF YOU ARE DEAF AND THE FLOOR IS MADE OF ~~SPONGE~~ SPONGE."

"IS THIS GOOD(?)" BRYAN ASKED AND HE OPENED AN OLD CAKE TIN. I PEERED INSIDE AND SAW A HUGE BLUE, BREATHING JELLYTOT WITH ONE EYE AND A MAN'S PENIS SEWED ~~ONTO~~ ONTO ITS CHEST. LIKE BLUE MEAT SPRINKLED WITH ICING SUGAR.
THE THING LOOKED UP AT ME AND SPRAYED GARDEN PEAS INTO MY EYE.
" IT'S FERRY GOOD," I SAID AND WE DANCED AND RAN AROUND ENJOYING OUR BODIES IN THE HOT AFTERNOON SUN.

BRYAN FERRY FELL ON TOP OF ME
LIKE A GIANT FOAM WARDROBE.
I STARTED TO SUFFOCATE UNDER
HIS GLAM ROCK TEXTURES.
IT WAS AS IF HIS FORM
WAS A SOLID THICK LIQUID,
LIKE MELTED SHOES
OR ONE OF THOSE SMOOTHIES
FROM TESCO METRO, POURED INSIDE
A MAN SHAPED RUBBER SLEEPING BAG.
IF I OPENED MY MOUTH HIS
LIQUID MASS FITTED INTO MY
CAKE HOLE FLUSH SQUEEZING OUT ANY
STRAY AIR AND ABSORBING
ME LIKE A HORROR BLOB.

BRYAN HAD COME SO FAR AND FELT HE
COULDN'T RETURN TO HIS HOME LAND. HE DREAMT OF
THE BUFFALO PEOPLE AND BUILT PERFECT GLASS CUBES A
HUNDRED FEET TALL AND DEMANDED THAT I FILL THEM
WITH CHEESY MASH. WHILE HE WAS AWAY AT THE BOOK MAKERS.
THIS WAS AN IMPOSSIBLE TASK. WE WERE LIVING IN A TIME
OF NO FIRE OR SAUCEPANS. I SMASHED THE
GLASS TANKS WITH A FROZEN KINGFISHER
AND SAT CROSS LEGGED IN SILENT PROTEST.
BRYAN FERRY RETURNED AND LOOKED HURT. HE DANCED AND
SWIVELLED ON THE BALLS OF HIS FEET, HALF CLOSING HIS
EYES, GIVING THEM THE ILLUSION OF BEING SPLIT PEAS.

I LAUGHED
HE LAUGHED

"SPAGHETTI" HOOPS LAUGHED
AND WE SUCKED UP THE BROKEN
GLASS THROUGH STRAWS LIKE
HOOVERS MADE FROM OUR
FORMER MEMORIES.

DONE

GORDON RAMSAY

Noel

BRYAN FERRY

BRYAN WORE AN EYE PATCH AND A BLACK LEATHER
POPES' HAT. HE HAD ATTACHED TIN CANS AND TENNIS
BALLS TO A YELLOW WASHING LINE.
BRYAN WAS BEING FOLLOWED BY BLACK SKELETONS
WHO CARRIED ROTTEN POLES AROUND WITH THEM
AND USED THEM FOR PUNTING DOWN THA RIVERS OF
CAMBRIDGE. RIDING A HOLLOWED OUT PANDA INSTEAD OF
A BOAT. THEY CALLED IT TRISHA
THE BATTLE SHIP.

YOU COULD HEAR THEM LAUGHING
AND CLICKING IN THE NIGHT.
BONEY MORONS.
WHO LIVED ON THE EDGE OF SOCIETY
AND DID THINGS JUST FOR SHOW.

BRYAN WORE A PAPER KILT
AND A SPRAYER WHITE
AFRO. HE CARRIED AN ALSATIAN
AROUND WITH HIM.
HE CALLED IT "SPAGHETTI HOOPS"
AND STARTED WEEPING,
MAKING SURE THE TEARS FELL LIKE
RAIN DROPS ONTO THE GUARD DOG'S
SOFT BLACK N BEIGE HEAD.

HE SCREAMED AT THE DOG
ASKING IT TO
DO HIS TAX RETURNS.
BRYAN NOTICED THE DOG
HAD TWO DARK PATCHES
ABOVE ITS EYES.
BRYAN SHOUTED "SPECIAL MARKINGS =
EYE BROW ILLUSION WALLETS"

BRYAN AND SCOTT
WALKER CIRCLING
THE BEACH,
SKIMMING THE
SURFACE OF
THE OCEAN WITH
WOODEN INSECTS,
DARTING EYES
NO SURPRISES
LEFT ON THE
CRAB SCUTTLING
DRIFT WOOD
PALACE.

Jellyfox

HACKNEY

Car visual / Screen behind us

Monkey Song

ws
Feature.

ws.)

Zebras

psychodelic

FLOAT

not red puppets

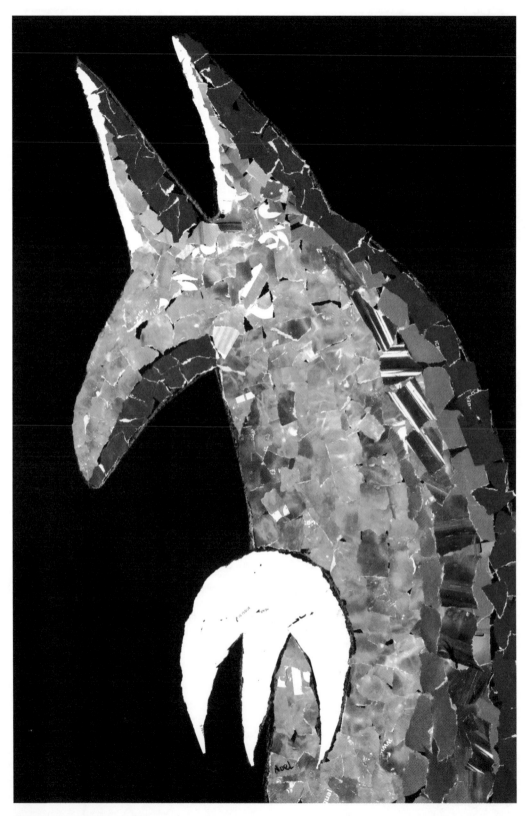

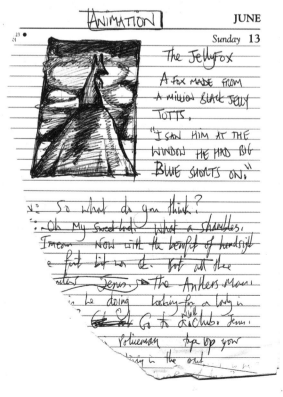

Sunday **13**

The JellyFox

A Fox made from
a million BLACK JELLY
TOTTS.

"I saw HIM AT THE
WINDOW HE HAD BIG
BLUE SHORTS ON."

v: So what do you think?
: Oh My Sweet Lord! What a shambles.
I mean Now with the benefit of hindsight
a first bit no it. But all these
Jesus. The Antlers Man
is he doing looking for a lady in
Go to a club, Jesus.
Policeman tape up your
in the out

MMMM OOMM

LITTLE CHRISSY

I AM I NOTHING

G II Z G III M

266

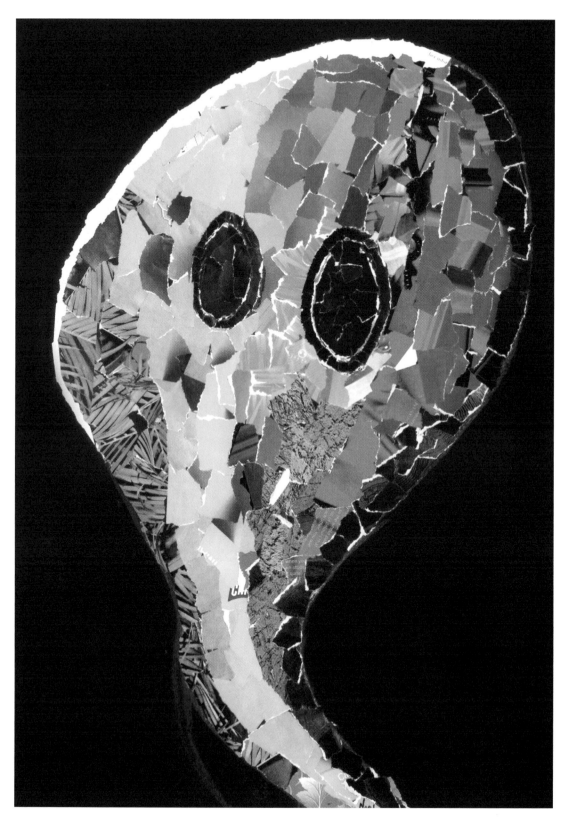

267

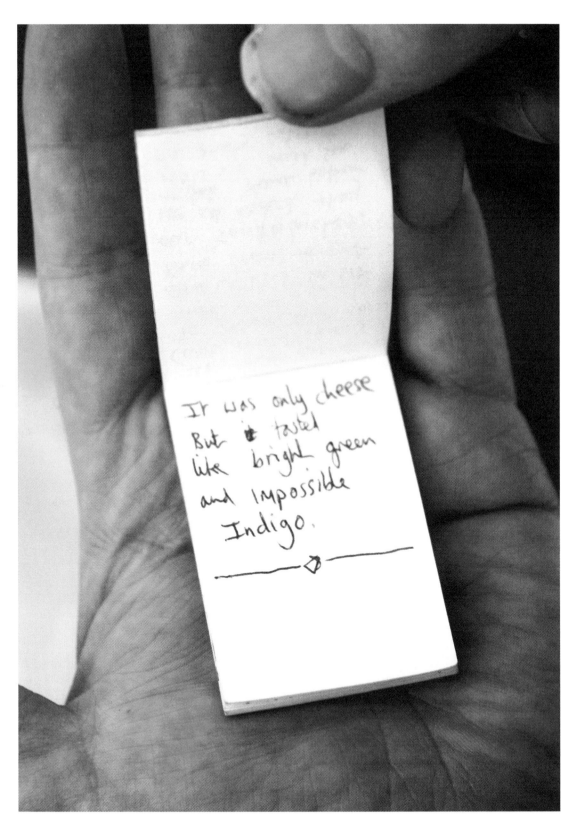

279

These
People
are idiots

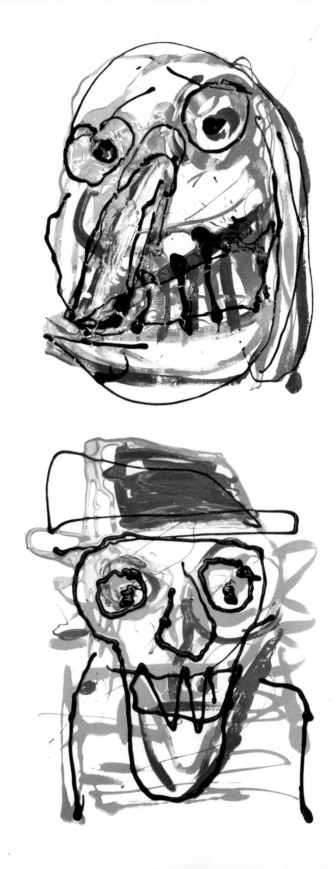